Tartuffe or The Imposter

**by
Jean-Baptiste Poquelin Moliere**

**Adapted by
Charles Jeffries and Luis Muñoz**

Baker's Plays
c/o Samuel French, Inc.
**45 West 25 Street
New York, NY 10010**
bakersplays.com

Tartuffe was originally produced by MacArthur High School, in San Antonio, Texas in the spring of 1988 for the Texas U.I.L. One-Act Play Competition. It was directed by Charles Jeffries and Luis Muñoz. Crew members were Tumu Rock, David Williams, Suzan Willey, Sarah Maymar, James Raddin, Richard Autry, Diana Anderson, Drucilla Martinez, Donald Ellis, Jarrod Polunsky, Henry Talamantez, Sonya Sokol, and Dawni Rios Alternates were Adam Vanek and Braden Hanna. The cast was as follows.

MME. PERNELLE .... Laura Harris
FILPOTE ....   Debbie Paredez
DOREEN .... Nicole Dewey
DAMIS .... Roger Sedarat
MARIANE .... Angela Tufts
ELMIRE .... Jenny Boring
ORGON .   ...John Poole
VALERE .... Brian Box
TARTUFFE ..   .. Jeff Tubbitt
LAURENT .... Eric Geyer
OFFICER OF THE KING/SERVANT   Coleen McGinley
SERVANT IN BROWN .... Matt Conner
SERVANT IN GREEN .... Erin Searcy
SERVANT IN PINK .... Ryan Reavis
SERVANT IN BLUE .... Michelle Jordan

CHARACTERS
6m, 5 f

MME. PERNELLE — Orgon's mother.
FLIPOTE — her maid.
DOREEN — a maid in Orgon's house.
DAMIS — Orgon's son.
MARIANNE — his sister.
ELMIRE — Orgon's present wife.
ORGON
VALERIE — in love with Marianne.
TARTUFFE — a hypocrite.
LAURENT — assistant hypocrite.
LOYAL — Officer of the King/Servant.
FOUR SERVANTS (two male and two female).

SCENE

Long ago. A stopover for the Comedy Italienne on the stage of
the Hotel de Bourgogne in Paris, France.

The adaptors would like to dedicate
this acting edition version
to all those who worked on the production.

TARTUFFE
OR THE IMPOSTER

(Music begins in the dark. As light comes up slowly in the center front only. We see an actor sweeping. Another actor is sleeping center behind him on a bench which is located at the point of the two platforms. An actress is just to stage left sitting on the steps. She has been working on a dress but has fallen asleep. As the actor sweeps, he turns and sees the audience. At that point a general low blue light begins to fill in the rest of the stage. He bows. The broom needs to be homemade and have a short handle, which makes his work the more difficult. After his bow he returns to sweeping. The actor on the bench rolls over and falls off his bench with a loud noise. At this point actors start entering from all over the stage, going to their places for the first action. The noise level increases. They are placing the ottoman on stage right and the table on stage left, adjusting costumes, placing props, and so forth. They are the Illustrious Company Comedy Italienne, a less than well-off touring company, getting ready to perform here at the Hotel de Bourgogne, Paris, France in 1679. The sweeper, at the right moment, beats his broom handle on the floor three times, the traditional way of beginning the performance in the French theater of this period.

They all come to the front or on the high platform center and on cue, all bow, traditional to the period. They then break very loudly and rush to where they belong for the beginning of the show. There is a GONG and the music cue stops and the show begins.

Lights up on the top of the platform and Mme. Pernelle, Orgon's mother, enters through the curtain as we hear a religious chant off stage by Tartuffe and Laurent. The chant drops in volume when the curtains close. Mme. Pernelle is coming in

7

from praying with Tartuffe. All characters on stage are frozen in a stance that will explain their character as they are activated by Mme. Pernelle.)

MME. PERNELLE. *(At center above, to the audience.)* Oh my dear, dear friends. Flipote and I must go. *(Break.)* No one cares to please me. Everyone shouts at once. No one cares the least bit what I think. No one shows me the slightest respect. It is like an enormous zoo. *(She imitates one slightly. Turns to the left and sees Doreen in pose on the step and crosses to her as she speaks the line.)* Doreen is nothing but a maid and much too much of a talker. *(Takes a handkerchief and stuffs it into her open mouth. She coughs and makes a move, then freezes again.)*

ACTRESS. *(On stage right, speaks this line while the action is taking place.)* ... She gives her advice on everything.

MME. PERNELLE *(Turns back to the right and on the platform end finds Damis in pose on the steps.)* Four letters spell you my dear grand-son Damis... *fool. (She crosses by him to his right.)* From the first time I saw him in his cradle I said to myself, "that child is a fool," and predicted him becoming a good for nothing. *(She pulls his cane from under his hand and he falls to his knees, loudly in great pain with a gong sound. He freezes. Lights go down center and up stage right. Marianne is frozen standing on the ottoman, having her hem sewn by an actor. As she goes over.)* Ah, my grand-daughter, Marianne...

ACTRESS. *(In dark stage left.)* ... the sister meek and mild...

MME. PERNELLE. You know still waters run deep but deep down you're as bad as the rest. *(She sticks her with a needle. She screams with hands up, the tailor [male] does an equally high scream and does the same and they freeze. Lights go down stage right and up stage left as she crosses to Elmire posing in a freeze stage left with a fan outstretched in her left hand.)* My dear Elmire don't take this wrong but everything you do. .

ACTRESS. *(Scrubbing floor stage left.)* ... is simply wrong.

MME. PERNELLE. *(Gesturing to right.)* She ought to set these two dear children a good example

8

ACTRESS. *(Stage right in dark.)* ... as their late mother never failed to do..

MME. PERNELLE. But she's extravagant, *(Removes fancy handkerchief in her cleavage.)* absolutely extravagant.

ELMIRE. *(Reacts to exposed cleavage.)* Oh, my. *(Places fan over herself.)*

(At this point general light comes on and we get the feel of the play's beginning.)

MME. PERNELLE *(At center.)* Perhaps I've been too frank... *(Everyone as they come alive say OH NO!! Everyone moves about the stage getting things in place as she crosses left.)* I do not mince my words when something is on my mind.

DAMIS. *(Crosses to center upon platform and saying very loudly.)* TARTUFFE.. *(Everyone shushes him. At that point it is quiet and we hear Tartuffe chanting offstage in the background. He covers himself and adjusts what he was going to say.)* ... would be pleased!

MME. PERNELLE. The man's a saint. *(They all begin to bow to her and back away. Damis looks through the curtains off. As he does, the volume of the chat increases and goes back down when the curtain is closed.)* He must be listened to, and if I hear a.. fool, like you *(Crosses to Damis.)* attack him, I may get very cross! *(Damis giggles and she kicks his cane out from under his hand and he falls, again.)*

DAMIS. *(On his knees.)* The man's nothing but a hypocrite!

MME. PERNELLE. *(She leans down to his face and says.)* Be quiet, you twit!

DOREEN *(Crosses to Damis and Mme. Pernelle crosses to curtain on the platform, ignoring her.)* Before I'd trust him or his man Laurent I would need a good guarantee.

MME. PERNELLE. I can't vouch for his servant. *(Pause as she opens the curtain and his religious chant swells loudly and stops as she lets the curtain go.)* But Tartuffe — you have my guarantee he's a good man. I'm telling you, the wisest thing my son has ever done is to take Tartuffe, whom God has sent here to save our souls, into the bosom of his family. *(A GONG sounds. Stage*

Freeze and lights all go out but center down front. Doreen crosses down into the light as she speaks.)

DOREEN. Orgon...

ELMIRE. *(Crosses down.)* ... my husband .

DAMIS AND Marianne. *(Cross down.)* ... our father...

MME. PERNELLE. *(Turns.)* ... my son...

DOREEN. ... used to be wise.

ORGON. *(Crosses in above Mme. Pernelle on platform.)* ... and I used to be such a sensible man. *(Then exits off.)*

DOREEN. He loves Tartuffe one hundred times more than his family...

DAMIS. ... calls him brother...

MARIANNE. ... whispers all his secrets to him. *(All cross down, bunch and squat to tell secrets.)*

DOREEN. I'd say you couldn't be more loving to a mistress.

(All laugh. Mme. Pernelle exits off through the curtains. Noise offstage of horse hooves coming up the drive.)

ELMIRE. My husband's here. *(Crosses, stops, and gains control.)* I'll wait for him upstairs.

DAMIS. *(Crosses to her.)* Sound him out about my sister's wedding, will you? *(Spits out his name.)* TARTUFFE is opposed to it. *(All freeze — lights down except stage right. Damis crosses into light.)* It is important to me as well. My sister loves Valene... *(Valerie crosses to him.)*

GROUP OF ACTORS. *(At stage left.)* ... and he loves her...

DAMIS. ... and I am in love with his sister, and if TARTUFFE... well it would break both our hearts. *(They all freeze, Doreen crosses down front.)*

DOREEN. Tartuffe again!!!

(Gong. Damis and Elmire exit stage right. Doreen crosses up to stage right on the platform. Lights go down on stage right and up on the upstage center platform as Orgon enters from upstage, offstage left. Servants babble and cluster around him on his entrance. Orgon shushes them and they go down on the

stage floor and down on their knees. We hear Tartuffe chanting offstage.)

ORGON. (*Crosses up to curtain, moans and turns to stage left to give his cape and cane to a servant and says.*) Doreen. (*She comes up behind him.*) DOREEN... (*As he turns he ends the word with his nose on hers. He stops.*) Doreen. (*Moves her and crosses stage right.*) I'm anxious to know if everything has gone well these two days?

DOREEN. (*At center.*) Two days ago the mistress had an attack of fever, felt quite nauseous all evening and couldn't touch a mouthful of her dinner. (*Orgon is only vaguely interested.*) We finally persuaded her to be... (*Elongates the word.*) ... bled... (*Orgon crosses to curtain and slightly opens it so we hear two notes of the chant by Tartuffe.*) ... and she felt better at once.

ORGON. (*Turns to her.*) And Tartuffe... ?

DOREEN. ... To make up for the blood the mistress lost, drank four large tumblers full of wine.

ORGON. (*Drops to his knees in prayer.*) Poor fellow!

DOREEN. (*Crosses down front while Orgon freezes in prayer.*) Fact is, Tartuffe's a man can spot a victim. He wheedles money by turning on his sanctimonious cant and with hands full and his pockets bulging, he turns on us and does his preaching. (*She freezes with hands in prayer.*)

ORGON. (*Finishes prayer and stands, sees Doreen.*) You know I don't like that girl... but Tartuffe. You'd be captivated by him. Ah, if you had only been there when we met. He'd arrive every day in church and kneel, meekly, right next to me and never failed to capture the whole congregation's notice with the enthusiasm of his praying. His servant, Laurent (*An ugly sound offstage.*) who is like a mirror image, told me about him, who he was, his poverty. Finally I was inspired to bring him here.

ACTOR. (*On ladder stage left. In dark.*) ... he disapproves of everything...

ORGON. Of course...

ACTOR. (*On ladder stage right. In dark.*) ... and he keeps a very close watch on Orgon's wife...

11

ORGON. Just to protect my honor...

ELMIRE. (*Crosses into light from right to Orgon.*) Tartuffe is far more jealous than he's ever been... (*She continues her cross and exits stage left.*)

ORGON. You have no idea of the fervor of the man. Ah. . but now I must speak with that daughter of mine. (*He exits up stage left.*)

(*Doreen comes alive realizing the problem. She begins to spin left and right, not sure what to do. She stops. During this, on stage right in front of the ottoman, Marianne and Valerie have brought a bench out which has a black curtain attached to the back of it so that anyone on the floor behind it is not visible to the audience and are seated on it frozen in a kiss. In addition, two actors can be on either side of the area between the bench and the ottoman, forming statues as if in or around a fountain. One actor could be on top of the ottoman, creating another fountain statue. Doreen runs to stage right and the lights come up on them as she enters.*)

DOREEN. Your father ... !!! (*Valerie starts to exit left.*) No!

(*Too much time has passed, and so Valerie jumps onto the bench and poises as a piece of statuary. Doreen knows this will not work so she pushes him and he falls behind the ottoman. There is the sound of a splash as if there were a fountain and pool area behind the ottoman. If it is possible, a small handful of confetti could be tossed up as if it were the water splashing. Orgon enters.*)

ORGON. Marianne, I have something to say to you. (*Looking at Doreen.*) Privately! (*Doreen crosses left but dawdles in ear shot. Marianne is seated on the floor at the end of the bench reading a book, or so it would seem. The book is upside down.*) Marianne . (*He turns the book right side up.*) I've always appreciated your obedience.

12

MARIANNE. I'm very grateful for your fatherly affection. (*Doreen wants to stay so she slowly crosses up and gets on the ottoman with the statue that is there, pretending to be one also.*)

ORGON. (*Sits on bench next to her.*) And if I'm to continue, you only need to provide me with what I want.

MARIANNE. I take pride in that.

ORGON. Good. What do you think of our guest, Tartuffe? (*She rises and crosses left, sputtering words that seem to be negative. Loudly.*) Be careful what you say.

MARIANNE. (*Re-gaining control.*) Oh, dear, well, I'll say anything you like.

ORGON. Well then, my dear... (*He stands and crosses to her.*) Why don't you say he has reached your heart (*Crosses to her left.*) and it would make you happy if I agreed to let you marry him?

(*Marianne begins to sob and turns back to the bench while Orgon goes to the left to make sure no one is hearing them. At this point Valerie comes up for air from the fountain and she pushes him back down under the water as Orgon comes to her.*)

What is it???

MARIANNE. Why would you want me to tell a lie?

ORGON. I want it to be the truth. Yes, my dear, I intend to make Tartuffe your husband. (*At this point Valerie comes back up for air and his head is between them. Orgon leans on his head and says.*) It's true, I had promised you to Valerie; but he's been seen more than once playing cards, and I suspect he may be a libertine Haven't seen a lot of him in church. (*He stands and crosses to stage left as Marianne pushes Valerie back under the water*) Though not exactly pretty, Tartuffe is like...

DOREEN (*Comes out of statue pose.*) A gargoyle off the side of Notre Dame.

ORGON (*Sputters and turns back as Doreen goes back to being a statue. He thinks Marianne has said it.*) Shut up. (*Crosses to her.*) Heaven smiles on Tartuffe. You'll live together, like two... (*Hears birds chirping*) turtledoves. You will never quarrel (*Crosses*

13

back left.) and you'll find that you can turn him into anything you please.

DOREEN. (*Coming alive again.*) A cuckold, for example.

ORGON. (*Aside to audience.*) I have never heard such insolence. (*Cross to her.*) I insist on your obedience (*He exits on line to darkness on the center platform.*) and your complete acceptance of my choice. (*At this point Doreen can stand it no longer. She steps off the ottoman where she has been a statue on to the floor where it appears she steps on Valerie and his head pops up, then over the bench on the floor.*)

DOREEN. I wouldn't be seen dead with such a pig for a husband. (*Orgon has returned and hears this line. He swings with his right arm and she ducks. He then raises both hands in a fist to strike her on the head but she steps aside, where upon he strikes himself in the groin and drops to his knees as a GONG sounds. He moans there. To Orgon on the floor.*) And if she had any guts (*Kisses him on the nose.*) she'd say the same. (*Marianne rushes to Doreen and they exit to the left side of the stage. Orgon rises slowly and crosses to bench on the line, having trouble getting his breath*) You hussy! She's going to marry him and nothing either of you can say or do will stop it.

(*As he sits, Valerie comes over the bench and spews out a mouth full of water, then takes a deep breath. As Orgon looks at him the lights go down on them and up on stage left. Doreen and Marianne are to the right of the table at left, Doreen has been holding Marianne and as the light comes up on them, Marianne drops to her knees in front of Doreen with a pitiful wail.*)

How can we take pity on you when you let someone propose this idiotic plan, without saying a single word against it?

MARIANNE A father's power is absolute.

DOREEN. If he thinks Tartuffe is so attractive, he's quite welcome to marry him himself. (*She lifts Marianne and takers her to the chair by the table and seats her.*) And good luck to him. Now Valerie has made his proposal Do you love him?

14

MARIANNE Passionately.

DOREEN. And both of you are impatient to get married.

MARIANNE. Yes.

DOREEN So, what do you plan to do about Tartuffe?

MARIANNE. (*A wail and stands up and crosses around the table. She sees the bowl of fruit and taking a banana, holds it aloft*) Kill myself.

DOREEN. That's wonderful. (*Takes banana and crosses stage left in front of table pealing the banana*) I hadn't thought of that (*Crosses around to Marianne and stuffing banana in her mouth. Being mean!*) I see I was quite wrong to try to dissuade you He's the most eligible match, nothing to be sneezed at. (*Crosses down front*) Those red ears. That nice florid face

MARIANNE (*Worried that she means it, crosses to Doreen, bringing her an apple*) Please, Doreen, I want your help.

DOREEN (*Takes apple, crosses left in front of table and puts down apple.*) No, no, a daughter must obey her father, even if he wants to marry her to an ape (*Picks up banana to mirror the suicide of before.*) You will not escape him now You're going to be TARTUFFED!!! (*Marianne runs to stage right and throws herself on the ottoman. Doreen realizes she has been too harsh.*) There, there I won't tease you anymore (*Runs to her at the ottoman*) Heaven knows how. (*Enter Valerie upstage into the light from center.*)

VALERIE (*Crossing to her and she sits up. He drops to his knees*) Marianne What are we going to do about this? (*He was a little hard in his delivery and Marianne didn't like it. She crosses to stage center on the platform*)

MARIANNE (*Crosses left to down front*) Well, then, I had better follow your advice

VALERIE. (*Turns startled.*) What? (*Crosses downstage right, wagging his finger in her face.*) I don't think that will be too hard for you

MARIANNE (*Wagging her finger in his face*) No harder than it was for you to give such advice.

VALERIE (*Crosses around her to stage left and up on platform*) I did so in the hope of giving pleasure

15

MARIANNE (*Crosses stage left up on platform to face him*)
Whereas I shall now follow it to please you (*They both give a sigh of resignation*) Ah (*They sit on platform up above the one they are on. A moment and they face each other and smile, then give each other a kiss and freeze. Doreen enters up stage through the curtain above them on the platform and seeing this...*)

DOREEN Ahhhhhh Well let's see how they can get out of this. (*Crosses downstage to audience, stage left*) I never saw such fools in my life! He would rather die than see her Tartuffe's wife, but here they scratch and spit like dog and cat But talk sense to lovers, I've more sense than that! (*Offstage Damis screams which scares Valere and Marianne and they run offstage on opposite sides. Damis enters upstage through the curtain and runs down to left with Doreen*)

DAMIS (*As he runs in*) I'll break every bone in his body I mean it Doreen!

DOREEN (*Pulls him to center as she speaks and sits him on the bench at center*) Take it easy Let your stepmother deal with him She has some kind of influence on Tartuffe Perhaps he's even smitten with her She's summoned him. Wants to sound him out about the marriage (*Crosses up to look off through the curtains as she speaks*) His servant Laurent says he's praying but he'd be down soon (*Crosses up behind him on the platform at center*) So please go now

DAMIS Why shouldn't I be here while they're talking?

DOREN They must be alone

DAMIS I wouldn't say a word to him.

DOREEN. You're joking We all know what a short fuse you have

DAMIS (*Blows up—loses all control*) No I can watch my temper!!!!!!

DOREEN Go on Here he comes.

(*Damis runs to the table left and pulling part of the table cloth off hides under it on the chair stage left of the table. Doreen tries to stop him but freezes up stage right of the table in a pose.*)

There is the sound of a quiet religious chant offstage when all is calm. Tartuffe and Laurent appear behind the curtain. Laurent pulls the curtain open and bows to Tartuffe. Tartuffe enters. He is dragging a large cross which trails behind him. It is light and about five feet long. He has on a shawl made of what appears to be animal hair. His hair is black, long below his shoulders and very straight. He carries an oversized set of beads made of wood with a large cross. Another cross is around his neck, also made of wood. He is dressed all in black but a very good material with a bit of sparkle. Laurent is a carbon copy but no glitter. As he enters all actors on stage "hiss" him quietly. He looks over the stage and sees Doreen. He lashes himself once with the "wooden" beads at center. Laurent slips in behind him. Laurent is a carbon copy of Tartuffe but with the normal brown hair. He is "a learner." Tartuffe stops center and speaks quietly)

TARTUFFE. My hair shirt Laurent, please put it and this (*The cross.*) away next to my scourge If there are visitors tell them I'll be at the prison (*Crossing himself.*) distributing what few coins I have (*He is holding an open bible. Laurent takes the things offstage and returns*)

DOREEN (*Crossing center*) Sanctimonious twit (*He slams book shut. She takes a seat on the bench center.*)

TARTUFFE (*Pulls handkerchief out of his pocket and delicately hands it down to her from the platform above*) Please, cover your bosom That kind of thing can give (*Crosses left on platform away from her*) rise to guilty thoughts.

DOREEN (*Stands and steps to right on stage floor.*) I can't see why you should get overheated I mean, I could look at you stark-naked and not be tempted by a single inch (*She closes fan in a cutting way*)

TARTUFFE (*Crosses down on the floor left opposite Doreen*) If you don't show a little modesty I'll be obliged to leave you (*He starts left*)

DOREEN (*Turns to him*) Oh, wait I have to give you a

17

message.

TARTUFFE. (*Stops and faces front.*) I have no time for messages (*Crosses self.*) Many unfortunate souls await me. (*Freezes.*)

DOREEN. From Madame...

TARTUFFE. (*Has a little shutter and tremble.*) Oh..! (*Cast all go "Uh..!"*) Madame Orgon?

DOREEN. (*Crosses to him and beyond.*) She'd like a word.

TARTUFFE. (*Counters her and faces her.*) By all means Immediately

DOREEN. But... (*Pause*) What about the unfortunate souls?

TARTUFFE. For a soul, time is of no account. (*Doreen laughs*)

DOREEN (*He freezes. She speaks to audience*) That's cheered him I think I must be right

(*Doreen crosses upstage right as Elmire enters. They give each other the sign. Tartuffe throws his book to Laurent on the platform who exits and turns away for Elmire's entrance. She clears her throat when she is in place and he speaks*)

TARTUFFE. (*As he turns to Elmire he chants this line and drops to his knees in front of her.*) May God in all his infinite goodness grant you perpetual health in body and soul. . (*Pause. Like a little child.*) and bless you!!! That's this humblest suppliant's prayer.

ELMIRE. (*Not sure how to start speaking with him, she reaches to help him up but settles by patting him on the head like a dog.*) I'm very grateful. (*She crosses to the ottoman at stage right and, patting the seat next to her, says.*) Sit down. (*He moves quickly to sit by her... very close.*) I've been wanting to talk to you in private. I'm glad we are here alone. (*She doesn't know that Damis is under the table cloth on the chair far stage left.*)

TARTUFFE Yes, I'm delighted. (*She fans.*) It is such a pleasure to be alone with you for the first time. (*The intensity

18

builds as he finished this line to an explosion at the end) An opportunity I've often... (*His knee begins to shake out of control.*) prayed for.

ELMIRE. I thought we could just have a *conversation*... in which you'd feel you might confide in me (*Damis moves under the cloth.*)

TARTUFFE. And I want nothing better... (*Puts hand on her hand*) than the chance, the privilege... (*He's squeezing her hand very hard.*) of baring my soul to you

ELMIRE Oh, that hurts!

TARTUFFE. (*Stops and removes hand.*) It's just over-eagerness I never meant to hurt you, I'd much rather (*Puts his hand on her knee*) How soft and lovely!!

ELMIRE. What are you doing?

TARTUFFE Just feeling your dress. Isn't it velvety?

ELMIRE. Oh no, please don't. I am very ticklish (*She rises and crosses down front center. He comes behind her feeling the lace on her shoulders.*)

TARTUFFE. What workmanship! It's wonderful the things they do these days My word, I've never seen anything like it (*He could be talking about the lace but is he?*)

ELMIRE. (*Crosses left.*) I'm sure But can we get back to the point? I've heard my husband wants to give his daughter to you

TARTUFFE. He said something about it (*Crosses to her*) but all my desires are concentrated on a different set of wonderful attractions. (*Crosses behind her again.*) My thoughts, my dreams... (*This too has to build.*) my longings, my hopes. . (*He grabs her but she ducks left and he falls on his knees and it hurts.*) my tortured hopes.

ELMIRE. You mean you have no time for earthly matters.

TARTUFFE. (*On knees, turns to her.*) My heart is not entirely made of stone and our senses can easily succumb under the spell of God's perfect creations I can't look at you, you perfect creature, without admiring God's loveliest self-portrait Oh, at first, I was afraid this secret passion was a cunning subterfuge

19

of the Prince of Darkness, and I even determined to avoid you. But finally I realized, my sweet beauty, in such feeling there could be no guilt, it could be reconciled with purity, and that's when I surrendered myself to it *(He grabs her legs and she can not move. She reaches over him to his right shoulder and taps it with her fan. He thinks he is being interrupted and says.)* WHAT??? *(She rushes to get the table between them. He stands.)* Madame, I am not an angel and if my declaration is blameworthy, the real culprit is your enchanting beauty If you could bring yourself to show some favor, out of kindness, offer me relief. *(He has gotten behind her and is placing the large beads around her neck)* I guarantee my eternal, unparalleled devotion. *(Turns and begins to walk around the front of the table and the beads force her to follow behind him, closely)* Your reputation would be safe with me. People like us know how to love discreetly, and how to keep it permanently secret. Our own concern for our good character acts as a guarantee for those we love and once you've given way, you'll find we offer love without scandal, *(He turns to face her very closely.)* pleasure without fear

    ELMIRE *(She faces him and with deliberate threat in her voice.)* Aren't you worried that I might decide to tell my husband about this proposal? *(She removes the chain from her neck and crosses Down left folding her arms)* And that if he were told about your hopes it might do damage to his friendship for you?

    TARTUFFE. *(Realizing that he has gone too far, dipping slightly and recovering)* I know that you are too generous for that, and *(Crossing behind table left of Elmire who counters back to right of table)* that you will forgive my recklessness. *(Drops to his knees and begins to pray in what is Damis' lap on the chair.)*

    ELMIRE *(Crosses around to him)* Others might take another line perhaps, but *(Leans on Damis' head under the cover)* I prefer to exercise *(Pulls off the cover and sees Damis's face. Tartuffe does not see this as he is in deep prayer... she speaks this word to Damis)* DISCRETION!!! *(She recovers his face and crosses left in front of the table)* I shall say nothing of this to my husband, but in return I'd like something from you *(Tartuffe rises and sits on Damis' lap thinking it is the chair*) I want you to support, quite openly, Valere's marriage to Marianne, and to give up your unfair influence and your desire to enrich yourself... (*At this point Damis explodes, grabbing Tartuffe and standing up, throwing him on to the floor down front and straddling him.*)

DAMIS. No, no, everyone must know about this (*Pulling Tartuffe's head back while sitting on him. Tartuffe is not sure what is happening and is amazed. Elmire is trying to calm him down.*)

ELMIRE No, Damis. (*Everyone freezes in a distorted physical and facial way. All lights go out but one on Damis as he crosses down to the front.*)

DAMIS This liar has led my father by the nose for far too long, and done his best to undermine my love as well as Valere's Now heaven has afforded an easy way of unmasking the traitor. (*Jumps back on him, action returns.*) I have to take the opportunity

ELMIRE. Damis ..

DAMIS No, please, I have to trust my judgement. (*Orgon enters from up right and stops on platform*) Father (*Grabs Tartuffe by the hair and drags him to stage right on floor below Orgon.*) I've just caught this man making a proposition to your wife. You know her gentleness and her discretion; she wanted very much to keep it secret, (*Throws Tartuffe down and crosses back to stage left*) but I just can't indulge his shamelessness (*Crosses around to back of table as Elmire crosses down front on line.*)

ELMIRE. (*As she crosses down front.*) It's true I don't think one should ever ruin a husband's peace of mind for trivial reasons. Honor is not affected. (*Crosses on to the left.*) It's enough for us to know how to defend ourselves That's how I feel (*Crosses to Damis up of table and hits him with her fan.*) and if I'd had the slightest influence on you, you would have kept quiet (*She exits offstage left.*)

ORGON (*Crosses to him on floor and kneels behind him.*) Can it be true?

TARTUFFE. Yes, brother (*Orgon stands and slowly turns and crosses Up stage. Damis counters to center*) I wouldn't have the

21

arrogance to deny whatever (*Crawls on knees left to table.*) sin it is that I'm accused of. So fuel your anger, believe what they say, and throw me on the street... (*He prepares for the worst.*)

ORGON. (*Turns and slowly crosses straight down front*) You wretch, how dare you (*Turns and grabs Damis by the lapels*) fabricate this lie and try to (*Forces him to his knees.*) blot his virtue and purity?

DAMIS. You mean...

ORGON. Quiet!!!

TARTUFFE (*On knees left, not believing his luck but accepting it*) No (*He stands at table*) Let him speak Believe what he says. Why should you favor me? (*He starts to flagellate himself and run around the table to his right. Orgon follows him and Damis follows him. Once around and Tartuffe reverses and scares Orgon and Damis who then flee him.*) Come on, boy, call me a traitor, a lost soul, a degenerate, a thief, crush me with vile names. (*He has crossed to center, stands Down front and falls as if in a fit*) I deserve them all!!!

ORGON. (*Pours water from table and speaking to Damis*) Aren't you ashamed, you wretch?

DAMIS. (*At the right of the table.*) You mean you believe this hypocritical sinner? (*Crosses to left of Orgon and Tartuffe on floor*)

ORGON. (*Offering water to the prone Tartuffe*) Be quiet. (*To Tartuffe.*) Brother.

DAMIS. Maybe ..

ORGON (*Stands and throws water in Damis' face*) Shut up!

TARTUFFE. (*From the floor.*) Brother, I'd rather suffer any punishment than see him take a scratch on my account

ORGON. (*Damis and Orgon start to make up, we think. Both throw their arms open and move toward each other but Orgon grabs Damis by the neck and strangles him*) You upstart!

TARTUFFE. (*Gets on his knees*) Forgive him (*He starts to pray.*)

ORGON. (*Crosses over behind Tartuffe and Damis crosses left of the table*) See how kind he is, you louse

DAMIS. But...

ORGON. (*Crosses to table*) Silence!

22

DAMIS. What? I...

ORGON. I said silence *(Strikes top of table.)* I know your motives for attacking him. *(He crosses around table and Damis counters with the table between them)* No method is too brazen when it comes to driving this *good person* from my house Well, I'm going to give my daughter to him.

DAMIS. You're going to .

ORGON. Yes, wretch, and, to spite you, this very evening *(Cross back around table.)* Ha, I defy you all I'm going to teach you that I'm in charge here and I'll be obeyed So take back what you said this very minute *(Takes Damis' ear and forces him to Tartuffe's left, on his knees.)* Down on your knees and ask him to forgive you *(Orgon is on his knees right of Tartuffe)*

DAMIS Who, me? Me ask this unscrupulous fake ?

ORGON. *(Tartuffe is between them smiling at Damis and then looking innocent to Orgon alternately)* So you refuse, you ruffian, and insult him? *(They both stand)* Out of my house and don't you dare come back I hereby disinherit you

(Damis stomps off left and Orgon follows him as far as the table Tartuffe sneaks up onto the platform at center with his back to us. As Orgon returns he turns with his arms outstretched and the lights all go down but on him. Perhaps Bach could be played in the background. Orgon drops to his knees)

TARTUFFE *(Screams)* Do you see how much it hurts when people try to blacken me in your eyes .

ORGON Don't

TARTUFFE. Just to think of the ingratitude is such a cruel torment to my soul The horror of it . I can't speak *(He begins to waver as if to faint)* I see no alternative to my leaving *(He falls forward and is caught by Orgon, who turns and places him in his lap on the bench, ala the Pieta.)*

ORGON You think I'm going to listen to them? I defy them all *(Tartuffe begins to crawl on knees, left. Orgon stands)* and to show them what I think, I'll make you my sole heir and hand over all my worldly goods Won't you please accept my offer?

TARTUFFE (*Extends hand back to Orgon who places his keys into his hand. From our "angle" we see a big smile come to Tartuffe's face*) God's will be done One sacrifice after another That I should be burdened with possessions (*He begins to pray*)

ORGON. Oh, you humble me. Come, let us go and draft the papers, and let that jealous lot gag on their own spit! (*He turns to the right and begins to pray. Tartuffe turns to the left and looking over his shoulder makes sure that Orgon is busy praying. He rises and crosses left and the lights go down on Orgon. He speaks to the audience*)

TARTUFFE Those who know me would never dream of thinking that this is a result of my self-seeking. The riches of this world have very little appeal to me. I'm not one to dazzled by their illusory glow. (*Throws keys on table*) And if Orgon wants me to have this gift and .. I decide to take it. . (*Enter Laurent at center door very slowly*) Unwillingly, most unwillingly, it will only be because otherwise, to be honest, I'd be worried in case all of that money were to fall into the wrong hands and end up with people who'd use their share for evil purposes, rather than keeping it, as I intend to, for the glory of God, (*Laurent has crossed to him*) and the welfare of my neighbor (*Hand Laurent bag of coins. A bell rings twice offstage.*) You must excuse me now, it's half-past-three and I'm required upstairs to fulfill.. (*Weighs money pouch*) "certain religious duties " Much as I hate to leave you (*He and Laurent walk up to door chanting. On the platform he drops the keys and stops to pick them up and, facing Laurent, they say in a very devilish way, very loudly*)

TARTUFFE AND LAURENT AMEN!!!!! (*Gong and they exit.*)

(*Lights go down on center and come up on stage right ottoman. Marianne is lying on the ottoman face down, on her left is Elmire, on her right is Doreen. Orgon has gone up on the platform center and as the lights come up he speaks*)

ORGON Marianne (*Doreen crosses to Down stage right and*

24

Elmire crosses upstage left. Both are facing away from Orgon.) Oh, good! I'm glad I've found you all together. (*He crosses to Marianne and tries to show her the paper*) Now here is something which should raise a smile. This contract. (*Gets down on his knees to show it to her.*) You must know what it is about (*She screams and wails. The other woman come to her and Orgon crosses to center down. As soon as all the women are together they speak.*)

ALL WOMEN. You.. man!!!!!!!!

ELMIRE. (*Crossing down to Orgon.*) I'm staggered by your blindness You must be infatuated and obsessed with him, to overlook what's happened here today.

ORGON (*Turns to her.*) That Tartuffe had been making love to you? Do you expect me to believe that? (*Crossing up on the platform center*) Words, words, words. Words are heard . not seen Seeing is believing, and with all due respect. (*Starts to exit out center door*)

ELMIRE (*An idea dawns on her*) But if I could make you see we were telling the truth?

ORGON See? (*Turns and listens*)

ELMIRE. Yes

ORGON Rubbish! (*Exits through curtains.*)

ELMIRE (*Screams and becomes insistent.*) This delusion has lasted far too long, and I am tired of being accused of lying It's high time I gave myself the satisfaction of showing you everything we've said is true (*All ladies applaud*)

ORGON (*Crosses back in on platform.*) All right, I'll take you at your word. Let's see you keep your promise

ELMIRE. (*Turns to Doreen*) Bring him here to me

DOREEN. (*To Elmire*) He's cunning and he may not be so easy to catch out

ELMIRE. No; in love, deceit is easy (*Adjusts shoulders of her dress lower*) Vanity leads people to fool themselves Bring him, now (*Doreen exits. She turns to Marianne*) And you had better go (*She exits. Lights go down on area stage right and up on stage left. She crosses over the platform and leading Orgon to the table left*) This table (*She hits it with her fan.*) Get underneath

25

ORGON. What?

ACTOR. (*Offstage left, strongly.*) Do what you're told

ORGON. I must say, (*Crawls under table, she gives him a little kick.*) this is really very silly, (*He comes out the front of the table cloth on his knees and speaks.*) but I can't wait to see you prove your point.

ELMIRE. I don't believe you'll have any complaints (*He is still visible at the front of the table.*) I shall coax, (*She starts to clear table of anything on it, candles, etc.*) since I'm reduced to this, this hypocrite will take his mask off, and I shall encourage his insolent desires and stimulate his recklessness (*Everyone applauds.*) Since all this is for you, I'll only stop it when you acknowledge you were wrong, so things will go as far as you allow them. (*Tartuffe and Laurent enter through curtain and pause.*)

TARTUFFE. I'm told you asked to see me (*She stomps on Orgon's fingers and covers him with her dress until he has gone back under the table unseen.*)

ELMIRE. (*Crosses to center.*) Yes, there's a secret I must tell you. (*She lifts her dress to show her ankle. Laurent rushes down on her left side and Tartuffe does the same on her right side. They make appropriate noises as they do. She turns to Laurent and hits him with her fan and he retreats up and out the center door. She then turns to the right and addresses Tartuffe.*) Before I do, would you please make sure that no one surprises us (*He runs upstage right on platform to look out the door. She does the same thing upstage left. They look out and then turn face to face. She uses her fan to caress his cheek.*) Now I reveal to you what I should perhaps have kept back a little longer. (*She crosses stage right on platform and she turns to him. He counters left.*) I throw all modesty to the winds. I lay bare my heart I confess not only my love, but my willingness... (*Both cross as close as possible to each other at center. Then he takes one step back.*)

TARTUFFE I'm not quite sure I follow you, Madame Just now you gave a very different answer (*He crosses behind her to right and down on to the stage floor and turns to him.*)

ELMIRE. You must know very little about women. Our

26

voice, for virtue's sake, protesting feebly against our instincts, gives the kind of . "no"... which promises everything

TARTUFFE. (*Deep breath and they cross to each other center*) To hear such words from such a lovely mouth is exquisitely pleasurable, Madame. But what do I hear... (*Backs her up on these words step by step to the table which stops her retreat.*) Words, words, words. (*Putting his arms around her.*) How can I believe those words, unless they are translated for me... by deeds. (*She laughs and escapes under his arm and crosses over by steps*)

ELMIRE. Oh, you men! Very well. The man who is not satisfied (*Addressed to Orgon, loudly*) with words, shall have the proof he desires. (*Cross up on platform. He follows*) But how can I agree to what you want without, as you would say, offending God?

TARTUFFE. (*Crossing very close to her.*) I can dispel these ludicrous alarms, I know the art of (*Removing her fan from her cleavage*) freeing inhibitions (*Leads her downstage center*) I'll be responsible for everything and take the sin upon myself, Madame. (*He pulls her into his lap on the bench. She does the old fan-on-the-opposite-shoulder trick again and he turns and says*) WHAT (*She then escapes and crosses to table coughing and finally banging on the table with each cough*) That is a bad cough

ELMIRE Yes, it's misery (*She kicks under the table and is rewarded with a howl from Orgon.*)

TARTUFFE. (*Crosses to her and lifts her up in his arms.*) Anyway, I can easily remove your scruples This will be completely secret Sinning in silence . (*He has her on the table and is on his knees over her*) is no sin at all

ELMIRE. (*Who is trapped*) My husband... (*This scares Tartuffe who leaps off her to the back and under the table as and Orgon comes out of the front of the table and stands. Make sure Orgon's legs are far apart.*)

TARTUFFE. (*His head comes out front between Orgon's legs. Orgon freezes.*) Why worry about him? Between ourselves, he's easy to manipulate (*Orgon gingerly lifts his leg over Tartuffe and goes to the left side of the stage*) He takes pride in our relationship I've

27

got him so that he wouldn't (*He turns up to Elmire.*) believe it even if he saw us

ELMIRE Words, words, words Go and have a really good look out there (*Tartuffe rises and crosses to door, not seeing Orgon at stage left*)

ORGON (*To Elmire*) So you were right

ELMIRE. (*Swings around and sits on the table.*) Already! Get back under the tablecloth, (*Slaps the tablecloth.*) wait till he's finished I don't think you should make any unfair assumptions

ORGON (*Comes down to table and sits on the right side of it*) He's worse than any devil out of hell (*Tartuffe enters and is still looking off. Elmire hides on the left side of the table and Orgon just lies back on the table. It would be best if they were wearing the same color costume for this but to work well, in the mind of the audience*)

TARTUFFE I've checked all around, there is no one . my delight (*He lets out a whoop and runs to the figure on the table and jumps on the down stage side of Orgon. This is when Orgon slowly rises and Tartuffe slowly comes up face to face with him. Also, Elmire rises into view at the same time behind Orgon*)

ORGON I wouldn't let yourself get too excited (*Turns back to Elmire*) I think we have enough proof .

TARTUFFE You mean you think ..

ORGON Oh, please Now take yourself off me without further ado

(*Tartuffe gets off the table and crosses dejectedly to the top of the platform. Orgon rises and stands down stage of the table with Elmire to his left.*)

TARTUFFE. (*Turns and crossing himself.*) I never meant

ORGON Get out of my house!

TARTUFFE (*Rising in anger and no longer afraid*) No you get out of *my* house now. Attacking me is more dangerous than you think I have a way of punishing impostors, avenging this insult to God and making people who try to throw me out repent (*He turns and closing the curtains exits*)

ELMIRE (*Orgon crosses to center as the lights go down in stage left and up there.*) What does he mean .. this is his house? (*Crossing to him.*)

ORGON (*Turns back to her.*) I fear that deed of gift was a mistake.

ELMIRE. What deed of gift?

ORGON. (*Remembering and excited.*) The case.. !!!!!

ELMIRE. What?

ORGON The attaché case

(*They turn to one another and freeze holding hands. A bell starts to chime and actors, four to begin with but others as the lines are said, enter and form around Orgon and Elmire. They enter in time to speak their line and form a group around them. These lines are addressed to the audience. Everyone in the cast should have a line or more and they should all wear commedia masks but no other changes in costume, etc.*)

ACTOR ONE. A very old and very dear friend of his...

ACTOR TWO. Who was in trouble with the King. .

ACTOR THREE   left a case with him in strictest confidence

ACTOR FOUR. For upon it contents his whole future

ACTOR FIVE Perhaps his very life...

ACTOR FOUR Depended .

ACTOR SIX. To ease his conscience...

ORGON. (*Turns to audience*) I went straight to that traitor (*Drops to his knees.*) and invited him in...

ACTOR SEVEN Tartuffe persuaded Orgon to give him the case, on the grounds that if anyone ask.

ACTOR EIGHT. Orgon could deny he had it ..

ACTOR NINE And still have his conscience clear of any perjury . (*Bell chimes again*)

ACTOR TEN Such a heavy cloak of virtue is worn to conceal the vices beneath it ..

ACTOR ELEVEN. And such men can be dangerous...
ALL. Faithless... Deceitful...
ELMIRE. (*On her knees next to Orgon.*) And full of revenge..

(*All clear during the last few lines. And Tartuffe enters upstage center in darkness and crosses to front of the platform, into the shadow.*)

TARTUFFE. Ah, yes, and when they stab, they stab with concealed blades... (*He turns upstage and says*) Amen!!!... (*Gong sounds. He exits as Damis enters calling his father's name.*)
DAMIS. (*In from stage right and Valerie in from left.*) Father, father, there's a warrant out for your arrest! Tartuffe is on his way here.
VALERIE. They will take you to prison.

(*He lifts Elmire up and begins to lead her left while Damis helps Orgon up and leads him right. All the lights come up and we see the entire household preparing to leave. They bring in large carpet bags and all is chaos. On the platform above is Tartuffe and Laurent watching the action. At the right moment, there is the GONG and the lights all go down except on Tartuffe on the platform. All the other areas of the stage are in blue. Everyone freezes in whatever they are doing. Orgon needs to be on the stage floor slightly right.*)

TARTUFFE. (*Crosses as he speaks to the steps stage right of the platform.*) Not quite so fast my (*Snarl*) friend In the name of the King, you are under arrest. (*He refers back to Loyal who enters through the curtains. He has a long cane and a sword. He crosses in center and then to the steps to the left. Upon his entrance everyone goes to their knees*)
ORGON (*Tartuffe goes back to center and Orgon rises and crosses upon the platform to confront him.*) Have you forgotten all my charity?
TARTUFFE No, I am well aware of how you have helped

me, (*Sneer.*) my friend... (*Small cross and point to Loyal.*) but my first duty must be to the King In that commitment I would sacrifice my friends, my wife, my parents and myself

DAMIS. (*Crosses up to comfort his father*) If he was so consumed, how come he held off making it apparent until we caught him molesting Orgon's wife?

TARTUFFE (*To Loyal.*) Officer. (*Crosses down to the front center and lights come up there.*) Why don't you put an end to all this whining and do what you were ordered?

LOYAL. (*Drawing his sword.*) Yes, I suppose I've waited far too long. (*Crosses to Tartuffe's back and taps him on the shoulder.*) I'm taking you immediately to prison.

TARTUFFE. (*Turns, amazed.*) Me, sir? Why sir?

LOYAL. (*Pushes him to the floor on his knees.*) I don't have to explain myself to you (*Places sword to his throat. Orgon crosses down level on the floor with Elmire at his side.*) Sir, you're living in the rein of a King whom no impostor's cunning can mislead By a supremely fitting stroke of justice, he let slip something which allowed the King to identify him as a wanted man. His Majesty also despises his vile disloyalty and ingratitude to you and only made me his subordinate to see how far his shamelessness would go. (*He reaches into Tartuffe's pocket and takes out a paper.*) By his command, this deed you can now destroy.

> (*He hands the paper to Orgon who tears it up. At this everyone cheers. Tartuffe, realizing his chance, bites Loyal's hand and takes the sword and, staying on his knees, swings it around and everyone retreats. He then turns the sword on Orgon but he hears Damis behind him draw his sword. He rises and he and Damis fight to the stage right area. Tartuffe drives him back to the ottoman and closes on him. Damis kicks him off with his foot and he retreats stage left to the table. He jumps on the table. [A note: an actor needs to be hiding to the left of the table to steady it for him.] Damis is lying on the table and Tartuffe is going to stab him in the back. Laurent, who has been up by the door for a while, has moved down and*

31

at this point is behind Tartuffe. He taps him on the shoulder and as usual Tartuffe turns and says "WHAT." He sees that Laurent is holding a gun to his head and drops his sword. Everyone applauds. Loyal comes over and takes Tartuffe's right arm and Laurent takes his left and they lead him up to the center door. Laurent takes him out. Loyal turns and everyone bows, then he exits and all are happy. Orgon crosses to center and sits on bench. Doreen comes behind him up on the platform and says)

DOREEN *(Crossing herself)* Heaven be praised

ELMIRE *(Crossing and sitting by Orgon on the bench at his left, Doreen comes down and sits on his right on the bench)* A happy end

ORGON My humble thanks I send *(Goes to his knees and crosses self)* to the first of Kings We'll be a hundred times more loyal now Just one more thing, and all is reconciled. *(He crosses back to the left where Valerie and Marianne are standing. Marianne runs across the platform to stage right and Valerie drops to his knees expecting to be hit. Everyone screams. He gives Valerie's hand and lifting him, takes him to center front)* I give my faithful friend. *(motions for Marianne to come to him)* my loving child. May heaven's blessing on your pathway shine. *(To audience.)* Good joy to you and yours .. *(Turns to Elmire who joins him.)* and me and mine

(Takes her in his arms. They all bow as the chimes strike. They freeze. Lights go down except on the platform where we see Laurent on his knees praying. Orgon sees him and crossing to him lifts him and in animated conversation they move up to the center door. Orgon freezes and Laurent looks back at the audience and says in the evil way they have done before)

LAURENT AMEN!!!! *(Blackout.)*

* * *

SET

The set is suggested to be predominately in black and cream.

The table stage left is approximately 5'x5' and very sturdy so that actors may jump on it without fear or worry. The table cloth should be in two parts. the large under cloth should be in cream and fitted to the table all the way to the floor, the over cloth in black layered so that it comes down each full side in a point about two thirds of the way down. The cloth can be tacked to the table so that it is safe for the actors both on top and under the table

The poof is a balance to the table, on stage right It is about 4'x4' It is cream with a black material padding on the top

The bench center is cream with black padding It has a back on it that is about six inches taller than the platform behind it

Behind the two six foot pylons on stage left and right should be two ladders approximately six feet in height, on which actors may stand and observe the action of the play or comment from there when needed

Behind the curtain, between the two eight foot pylons on the upstage platform, a large cross may be in view with two tall candle holders on each side, upon which two candles burn throughout the play.

One 4'x4' platform placed at center with one corner pointing at the audience Once this has been placed all other elements are lined up on it. Going to left and right from this platform are two 8'x4' platforms and in the "v" behind these is another 4'x4' placed upon two four foot pylons on their side, for a base This will raise the back 4'x4' up above the front 4'x4' by one foot. Going off of this 4'x4' are two ramps left and right. Coming to these platforms are. Two small steps from the 8'x4' to the top 4'x4' at the corners, two large steps from the stage floor to the front 4'x8's at the junction of the front 4'x4' and the 4'x8's. Located on the two 4'x8's are two eight foot pylons standing, creating an opening leading off of the upper 4'x4' on to the ramps There are two six foot pylons at equal distances from the stage areas and offstage level to the ends of the corners of the 4'x8's. All of this should be played as closely as possible to the front curtain (approximately four feet back)

For lighting effects described here, you will need approximately ten controllable and dimmable areas and a general wash of blue for overall lighting.

COSTUMES

MME. PERNELLE — Dark, somber black or brown, very plain; approximately 60 years old.

DOREEN — Red dress with cream sleeves, mop servant hat; approximately 30 years old.

ORGON — Green trousers and green blue coat, good sensible dark gray wig, greyed small beard just on the chin; approx. 50 years old.

ELMIRE — Green dress, shows cleavage when pulled down from top of shoulders to over the shoulders; approx. 30 years old.

DAMIS — Little foppish, cream shirt and light pink pants and coat, carries cane, little over done; approx. 20 years old

MARIANNE — Peach dress, low cut, little over done, approx. 18 years old.

VALERIE — Dark peach coat and pink pants, good wig, bows on shoes; approx 25 years old, small

FLIPOTE — Spinster, dark brown dress, plain, not well to do, approximately 70 years old.

TARTUFFE — Black pants and coat with cream shirt, long straight black hair, a little sparkle in his costume but it is also black, no bows on shoes, approx. 30 years old.

LAURENT — Just like Tartuffe, but no sparkle. They should mirror each other. He could perhaps have a short black, straight wig, no bows on shoes; approximately 20 years old

LOYAL — Represents the King Strong red pants with a blue coat, colorful sash Very good and flashy wig, curls, sword and holder, bows on shoes, etc , overdone, approximately 30 years old

SHOES

All men must wear black, slightly high heel shoes, that are very shiny They should start practicing with them as soon as possible as foot noise of the actor is always a problem

Especially in farce: foot noise is not funny, just noisy

Ladies need very nice medium heel shoes to match their dresses. Bows would be all right on the younger women, not on servants

Other adaptations by
Charles Jeffries...

The Beggar's Opera

The Comedy of Errors

The Merry Wives of Windsor

Mistress of the Inn

Volpone